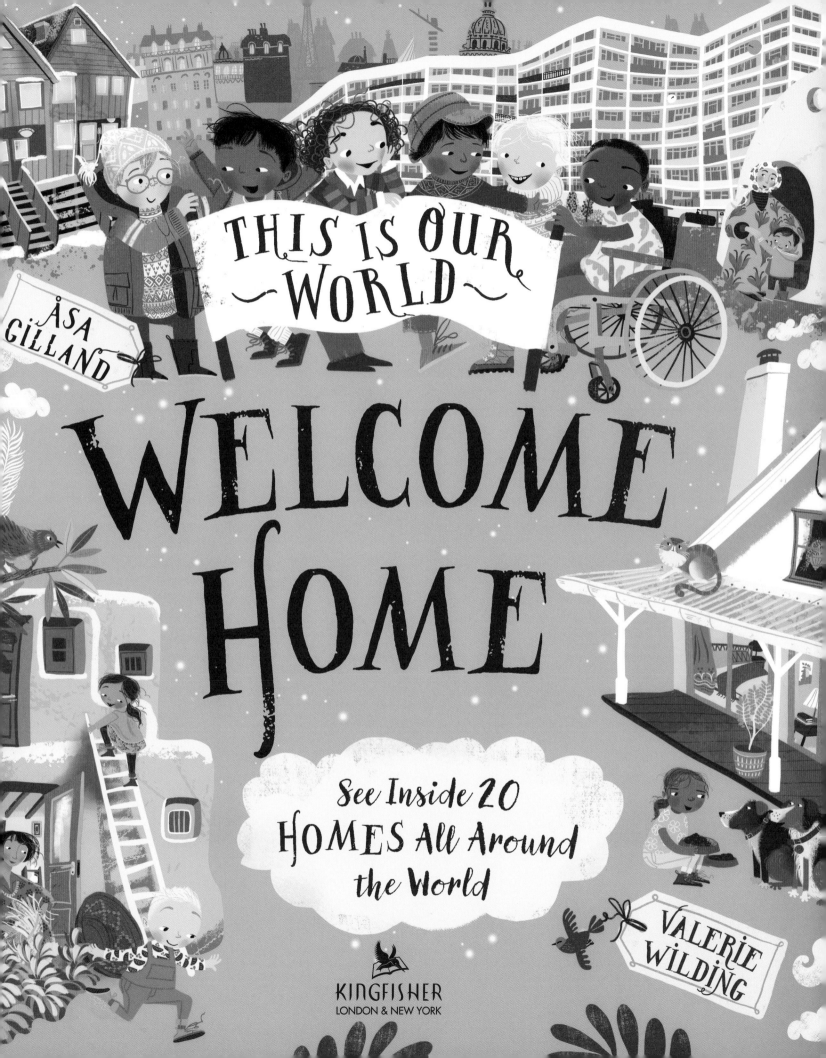

THIS IS OUR WORLD

ÅSA GILLAND

WELCOME HOME

See Inside 20 HOMES All Around the World

VALERIE WILDING

KINGFISHER
LONDON & NEW YORK

For Hettie James xxx —V.W.
For N., L., and G.—home is where you are. —Å.G.

Grateful thanks to Lyn and Gus Hughes,
and to Julie Sykes and Yeside Linney,
and to Reality Gives, Ghazala Irshad, and Sarah Clark

A Raspberry Book
Author: Valerie Wilding
Illustrator: Åsa Gilland
Editor: Tracey Turner
Art direction & cover design: Sidonie Beresford-Browne
Design: Nicky Scott

KINGFISHER
LONDON & NEW YORK

Distributed in the U.S. and Canada by Macmillan,
120 Broadway, New York, NY 10271

EU representative: Macmillan Publishers Ireland Ltd, 1st Floor, The Liffey Trust Centre,
117-126 Sheriff Street Upper, Dublin 1, D01 YC43

Library of Congress Cataloging-in-Publication Data has been applied for.

ISBN 978-0-7534-7970-4

Kingfisher books are available for special promotions and premiums.
For details contact: Special Markets Department, Macmillan, 120 Broadway,
New York, NY 10271

For more information, please visit
www.kingfisherbooks.com

Printed in China
1 3 5 7 9 8 6 4 2
1TR/0424/RV/WKT/140WF

CONTENTS

INTRODUCTION

The word "home" can mean all kinds of things—everyone will have a different picture in their mind. What do you see? Maybe a high-rise apartment, a cabin in a forest, or a cottage by the sea?

Whatever a home is like, they all provide us with the same things: a safe place to eat and sleep, and shelter from rain, snow, or desert sun. Home is a place where we can relax and have fun and be with the people we love the most.

The children in this book are going to show you their own homes, how they live in them, and the people and animals they share them with.

Some homes have many rooms, and others have just one. Some have a garden or more than one floor. They are on mountaintops and underground, in a desert and on farmland, even floating on a lake. Wherever they are, you'll be very welcome!

So turn the pages to visit homes from all around the world.

And watch out for the train!

STILT HOUSE, NORWAY

TERRACED HOUSE, ENGLAND

HAUSSMANN APARTMENT, FRANCE

ADOBE PUEBLO HOME, NEW MEXICO, U.S.A.

CAVE HOME, TUNISIA

FLOATING ISLAND HOME, PERU

SUBURBAN BUNGALOW, NIGERIA

TRADITIONAL MALOCA, BRAZIL

WHERE WE LIVE

HOUSEBOAT, THE NETHERLANDS

FALOWIEC APARTMENT, POLAND

OLD FARMHOUSE, GERMANY

TRADITIONAL YURT, KYRGYZSTAN

HANOK HOUSE, SOUTH KOREA

REFUGEE CAMP CARAVAN, JORDAN

DHARAVI SHACK, INDIA

RAIL LINE BUILDING APARTMENT, CHINA

HIGH-RISE APARTMENT, JAPAN

HONAI HUT, INDONESIA

MOKHORO HUT, SOUTHERN AFRICA

ECO FARMHOUSE, AUSTRALIA

ADOBE PUEBLO HOME

Hi, I'm Mila! I live with Mom and Dad in Taos Pueblo, New Mexico. Dad works far away a lot, and I love it when he comes home.

Taos is almost a thousand years old! We're Native Americans, with our own language—Tiwa—but we call our village by the Spanish word "pueblo," meaning "town." It looks as if someone built a row of rooms, then added another row on top but set back a bit, then more above that, like giant steps.

Our home is built of adobe bricks. They're made of earth, water, and straw, then baked hard by the sun. The earth contains a mineral called mica, which glitters in the sunlight. Long ago, Spanish invaders thought Taos was a city of gold!

RATTLESNAKE

COYOTE

WHERE: Taos Pueblo,
New Mexico, United States

WHO: Two adults
and one child

Taos means "Place of the red willow"
in the Tiwa language.

Mom and Dad's bedroom is next to
our living room, and mine is above
that. I climb a ladder to reach it. I have
a door opening on to the living room
roof, and I love stargazing outside.

We use oil lamps and
candles, as we have no
electricity, and we get
fresh water from Red
Willow Creek. It flows
a few yards from
our home.

MOCCASINS

Mom weaves basket platters in her
work room and makes moccasins
(shoes) to sell to tourists.

I catch the bus to school in Taos town. A lot of our neighbors
have moved there, where there's electricity and running water.
I'm very happy we live here!

RED WILLOW
CREEK

TERRACED HOUSE

Hey, I'm *Mark*. I live in Manchester in northern England, with my mothers, Mum and Mim. My brother, Sam, is in college. We live in a terrace—a row of houses all joined together.

Inside our front door there's a long hallway with stairs at the end. When we moved in, there were two small rooms and a kitchen downstairs. My mothers knocked down a wall to make one big room (me and Sam helped!). We eat at the table in the back half, and in the front half we watch TV sitting by the woodstove with our feet up.

TERRACE

I have posters of famous soccer players on my bedroom walls. Mum says my room's too cluttered to do homework in, but I always find a space.

WHERE: Manchester, U.K.

WHO: Two adults (sometimes three) and one child

Manchester has many terraces of houses like this one.

I love soccer, so the one thing I don't like about our home is that there's no room to play in the small backyard—only keepy uppies or kicking at targets on the wall. I play in the park with my friends, and if it's too wet we stay in and play video games.

BACKYARD

I ride my bike to school now, but when I go to secondary school, I'll get the bus. I'll have more homework than I do now, but my friends can still come over. The best thing about living here is having two friends who live in the same terrace and another in the house across the alley.

ALLEY

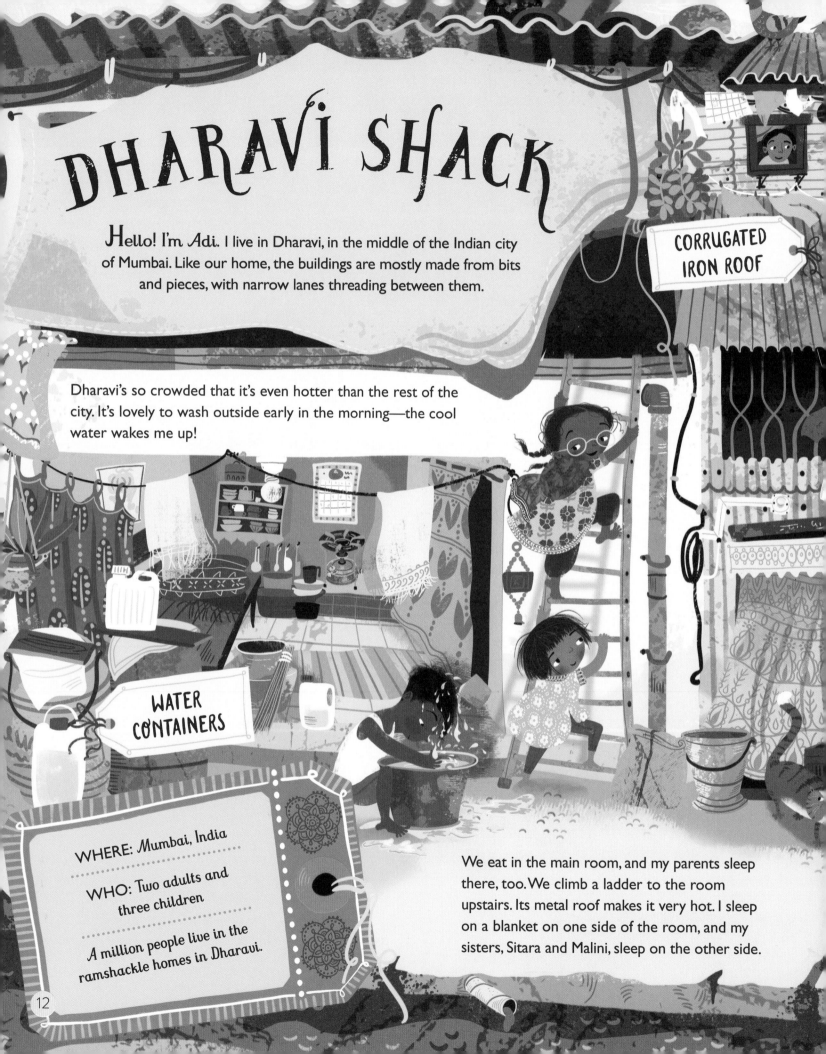

DHARAVI SHACK

Hello! I'm Adi. I live in Dharavi, in the middle of the Indian city of Mumbai. Like our home, the buildings are mostly made from bits and pieces, with narrow lanes threading between them.

CORRUGATED IRON ROOF

Dharavi's so crowded that it's even hotter than the rest of the city. It's lovely to wash outside early in the morning—the cool water wakes me up!

WATER CONTAINERS

WHERE: Mumbai, India

WHO: Two adults and three children

A million people live in the ramshackle homes in Dharavi.

We eat in the main room, and my parents sleep there, too. We climb a ladder to the room upstairs. Its metal roof makes it very hot. I sleep on a blanket on one side of the room, and my sisters, Sitara and Malini, sleep on the other side.

My father works for the best tailor in Dharavi, making suits for office workers. The workshop is on a wide, busy shopping street that runs through the middle of Dharavi. I walk along it after school.

TAILOR'S SHOP

Dharavi's noisy, hectic, and exciting, and always busy. People sell tasty snacks and fruit and vegetables, and recycling—you can get money for anything that can be recycled.

BASKET WEAVER

I stay on after school sometimes so I can use a computer. I study hard and I learn languages, which my teacher says will help me get a good job. I want to work at a bank and earn money for a laptop!

ECO FARMHOUSE

Hi! I'm Betty, and my sisters are Gabi and Lola. We're triplets, and we live with our parents on a small farm in Victoria, Australia.

WILDLIFE CORRIDOR

WALLABY

We're surrounded by farmland and forest, which we call bush. Over the years, my parents planted 7,000 trees and shrubs, creating wildlife corridors to help creatures cross our farm safely from one bush area to another. We helped!

KOALA

Koalas, wallabies, wombats, and possums live around us. And snakes! When we were little, we learned to check carefully before going through long grass. Lola once found one in the sandbox!

VERANDA

Our living room and kitchen are one big room, and we sisters each have a large bedroom. All our rooms have doors on to a shady veranda that helps keep the house cool.

EASTERN BANDY-BANDY

We use solar power. Rainwater runs off the roof into a tank for the house, and two small dams collect rainwater for our animals and veggie garden.

WHERE: Victoria, Australia

WHO: Two adults, three children, dogs, horses, cattle, and sheep

Remote farms like this one might be 20 mi. (30 km) or more from the nearest store, so being self-sufficient is important.

It's a long drive to meet the school bus, and we use some of that time for homework. After school, I go for a ride before feeding the horses.

WATER TANK

Lola feeds the hens and collects the eggs while Gabi feeds the sheepdogs. Dad deals with the cattle and sheep, Mum's the gardener, and I do the horses (the best job!).

At night I hear frogs croaking, owls hooting, and sometimes koalas grunting. In the mornings I hear lyre birds, and in the evenings gang-gang cockatoos visit our water troughs, squawking like creaky doors. We're lucky to live with amazing wildlife.

LYRE BIRD

FLOATING ISLAND HOME

Hello, I'm Alejandro, and my home's on a floating island on Lake Titicaca. I'm one of the Uros people, who have lived here for many hundreds of years. I live with Mami, Papi, and my baby sister, Maria, in a house made of totora reeds, which grow in the lake. We share our island with five other families.

Our island is made of totora reeds. Their tangled underwater roots form a thick mat, which we cut away from the lake bed. We attach the mat to wooden posts and stack layers of reeds on top to walk and live on. We keep adding fresh layers, so our island never gets waterlogged.

REED FURNITURE

Dried reeds are tied in bundles to make furniture and boats, called balsas. I made a little doll for Maria using totora. She wraps it in a tiny blanket, and I feel happy when she hugs it.

I go by boat to school on another floating island. Soon I'll go to secondary school on the mainland. The ground there is hard, not like our soft reed island. If we fall down playing soccer at home, we don't get hurt!

BALSA

Papi fishes and hunts. Mami cooks outside and sits in the sun embroidering cushion covers to sell to people who visit our islands.

WHERE: Lake Titicaca, Peru

WHO: Two adults, two children, two cats

Lake Titicaca is high up in the Andes mountains, 12,507 ft. (3,812 m) above sea level.

Our electricity comes from a solar panel. Papi has a cell phone, and Maria and I get to watch TV!

TOTORA DOLL

Our two island cats get plenty of fish to eat, and they make sure rats don't move in with us!

STiLT HOUSE

Hello, I'm Oskar, from Longyearbyen, on Spitsbergen island.
I live with my parents, my brother Mikkel, and the twins, Tiril and Tuva. Spitsbergen is
the largest island of the Svalbard archipelago, between Norway and the North Pole.

Our house stands on stilts! The soil is permafrost, which means
it's always frozen. If our warm house stood on the ground, its
heat would melt the permafrost and we'd sink.

Mikkel and I have our own bedrooms.
Our closets are enormous because outside
we need to wear thick coats, hats and
gloves, and lots of layers. It never gets really
warm on Svalbard, even in the summer.

WHERE: Longyearbyen,
Svalbard, Norway

....

WHO: Two adults, four children

....

Longyearbyen is the world's
northernmost town of more
than 1,000 people.

The sun never sets in the summer, so our
bedrooms have blackout curtains to help us
sleep. The winter is dark for months because
the sun is always below the horizon.

18

After breakfast, Dad drives to work on his snowmobile. He has to take his rifle in case he needs to fire it to frighten away a polar bear. There are more bears than people on Svalbard!

SNOWMOBILE

STILTS BEHIND HERE

Tiril and Tuva have tons of soft toys, especially kittens. Real cats aren't allowed here, to protect birds, like puffins, as well as other wildlife. Also, a cat might catch a dangerous disease, like rabies, from another animal and pass it to people.

PUFFIN

Mom's a writer. She takes the twins to school then walks back home to work. Most people leave their doors unlocked, so anyone can run to safety quickly if they see a polar bear. Mikkel and I walk to school on our own—unless a reindeer happens to keep us company!

TRADITIONAL MALOCA

I'm Taxli, one of the Tucano people, who have lived in the Amazon rainforest for thousands of years. My home is near the Vaupés River, where I live with my parents, three brothers, and many other relatives.

We share a longhouse called a maloca. There's a wide walkway through the middle, with doors to individual sections on the sides. We live in family groups of parents and children, and we cook and sleep in our own little section. Everyone shares the middle area. We're never lonely!

MALOCA

Some Tucanos have left their malocas to live in separate houses. Their community uses the maloca for ceremonies and for performing traditional singing and dancing for tourists. They sell craftwork there, too.

WHERE: Amazon rainforest, Brazil

WHO: 16 adults and 15 children

Malocas are made from wood with palm-leaf roofs and walls.

PINK RIVER DOLPHIN

We get plenty of food from the forest. We fish, or hunt with bows and arrows. And we grow plants around our maloca, like bananas, mangoes, papayas, pineapples, and a big bed of manioc, which we use to make flour.

MANIOC

PAPAYA

I speak several languages. Tucano people have to marry someone who speaks a different language, so in our maloca we pick up new languages whenever anyone gets married!

TOUCAN

Everyone worries about the damage that's being done to the rainforest. Big companies cut down trees to clear land for mining and farming. Cattle graze where forest creatures once lived. I wonder what will happen to us if the forest keeps being taken. It's our home.

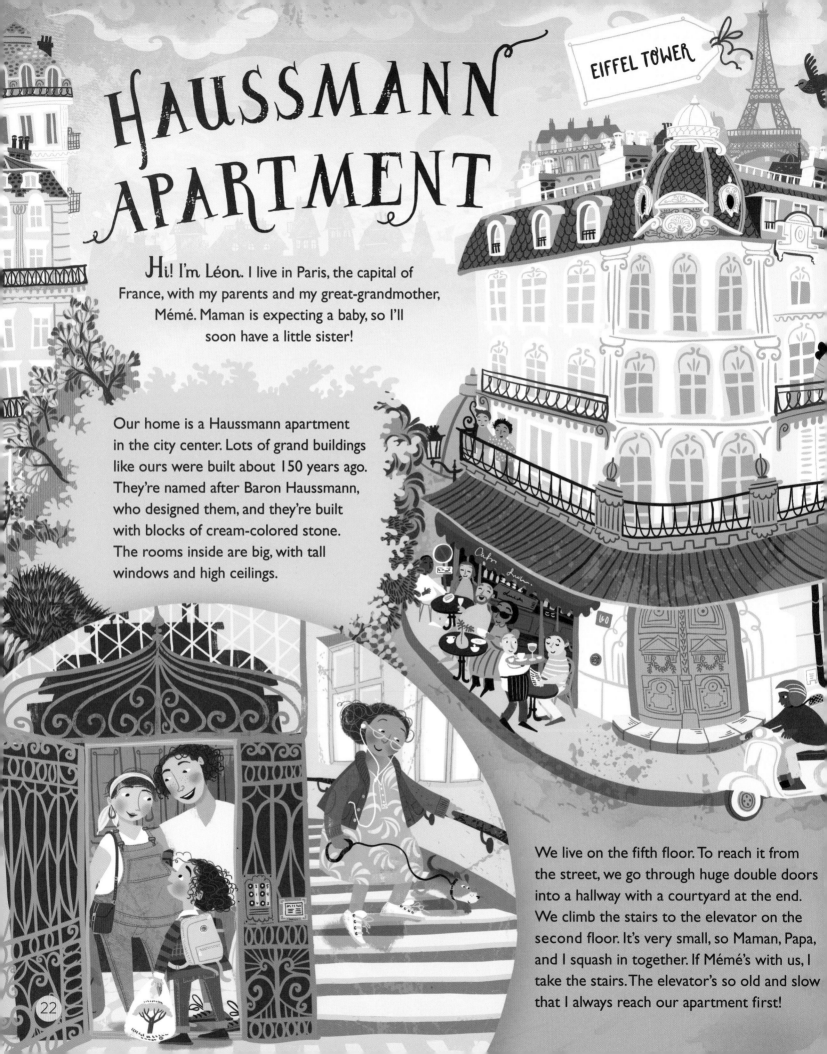

HAUSSMANN APARTMENT

EIFFEL TOWER

Hi! I'm Léon. I live in Paris, the capital of France, with my parents and my great-grandmother, Mémé. Maman is expecting a baby, so I'll soon have a little sister!

Our home is a Haussmann apartment in the city center. Lots of grand buildings like ours were built about 150 years ago. They're named after Baron Haussmann, who designed them, and they're built with blocks of cream-colored stone. The rooms inside are big, with tall windows and high ceilings.

We live on the fifth floor. To reach it from the street, we go through huge double doors into a hallway with a courtyard at the end. We climb the stairs to the elevator on the second floor. It's very small, so Maman, Papa, and I squash in together. If Mémé's with us, I take the stairs. The elevator's so old and slow that I always reach our apartment first!

22

We have four bedrooms. Mémé's overlooks the courtyard, so it's quieter than mine, and she lets me do my homework there. I hear traffic noise all the time in my room.

Our double windows open on to a long balcony with fancy iron railings. I love being out there, watching the buses and cars and people scurrying around. The cooking smells rising up from the restaurants below make me hungry! If I look left, I can see over hundreds of rooftops, and if I look right, I can see the most famous structure in France, the Eiffel Tower.

BALCONY

WHERE: Paris, France

WHO: Three adults and one child

Baron Haussmann designed his buildings on wide avenues, with parks for the residents.

HANOK HOUSE

Hello, I'm Sun-hee. I split my time between an ordinary apartment, where I live with my parents, and an extraordinary house where I live with my grandparents.

Both homes are in Seoul, the capital of South Korea. My parents work overseas for three months at a time, so then I come to live with my grandparents and aunt in their hanok house.

Hanoks are traditional homes made of wood and stone, with tiled roofs. Ours is in a hilly area called Bukchon. People love exploring the lanes and alleys lined with hanoks.

KOI CARP

Inside our entrance there's a small courtyard with a tiny pond that me and Grandma take care of. It has fish called koi carp in it, and I've arranged Grandma's pots of herbs around it to give them shade.

WHERE: Seoul, South Korea

WHO: Three adults, one child, lots of fish

Hanok houses like this one have existed since the 1300s.

My bedroom floor is lovely and warm because hanoks have heated floors, so that's where I sit to do my homework! At bedtime, I lay out my bedding and snuggle down. In the mornings, I fold it up and stack it in the corner.

SLIDING DOORS

My bedroom window has hanji paper instead of glass. The paper is treated with bean oil to make it waterproof, but it lets light in. There's hanji in the sliding doors between our rooms, too.

ACCORDION

Every week, my grandparents have friends over. Grandpa plays his accordion, and Aunt Mishil sings Korean folk songs. I watch TV with my headphones on!

I love summer evenings and Sundays, when tourists aren't allowed in Bukchon. Then I can explore and play outside with my friends.

SUBURBAN BUNGALOW

Hello, I'm Olufemi, and I live in Yaba, which is a suburb of Lagos, Nigeria. I live with my parents, my grandfather, my sister, Abi, and three brothers.

Our home is a modern bungalow. We moved here because my brother Jaja can't walk much. He has a wheelchair, and he can wheel straight into any room because there are no stairs.

We have three bathrooms, which is good, because we shower twice a day and there are a lot of us! Nigeria is hot, and the Yaba traffic is bad, so we often have a dusty journey home from school. Sometimes power cuts leave us in the dark, but we have a small generator that gives us electricity when that happens. Nobody wants to be in the shower when the lights go out!

There's a desk in the room I share with Jaja, where we do our homework. The rest of the house is always noisy with kids playing, Dad's terrible jokes, Grandfather grumbling, and Mama singing as she cooks mountains of food. Her jollof rice fills a dish the size of a small boat!

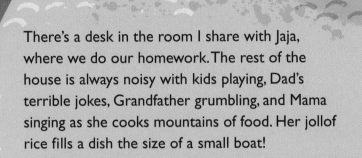

WHERE: Yaba, Lagos, Nigeria

WHO: Three adults, five children, one dog

About 16 million people live in Lagos—more than in any other African city.

JOLLOF RICE

Abi plans to be a police officer or a soccer player when she grows up. Jaja and my other brothers all want to be doctors. I'm going to travel all over my country, finding out about it, then I'll write a book called *Fantastic Nigeria*.

ANAMBRA WAXBILL

We have a big brown dog named Buzz, who lives outside. She is great at guarding our house!

FALOWIEC APARTMENT

Hi, I'm Tomasz, and I live in a falowiec apartment building in Gdańsk, Poland. Although it's only eleven stories high, there are 1,792 apartments, and about 6,000 people living here. The building is so long—2,790 feet (850 m)—that it has three bus stops, one near each end and one in the middle!

OUR APARTMENT

STICK INSECT

Our falowiec was built over fifty years ago. It started out as four buildings, but when they were joined up to create more apartments, it became a wavy shape. Its name comes from "fala," which means "wave."

I live with Mama and my brother, Janek, on the ninth floor. We all love animals, but Mama said we could only have pets that didn't need to go outside, so Janek chose hamsters. I chose stick insects. Mama said they're perfect because they're quiet and friendly, and they don't smell. Hamsters are not quiet. They play at night! The noise in our small bedroom used to wake us up, so we put them in the hall till morning.

Our living room has a door to the balcony, and we can see the sea from there. On sunny days, we meet up with my friend Monika from next door and walk through the park to the beach. Janek loves running around the grass and through the woods, so it takes us a long time.

WHERE: Gdańsk, Poland

WHO: One adult, two children, two stick insects, two hamsters

The Falowiec in Przymorze is the biggest apartment block in Gdańsk and one of the biggest in Europe.

SHOPS AND CAFÉS

It's great living in the city, and it's even better to have a park for picnics and skateboarding, as well as a long, sandy beach to play on. We're so lucky!

MOKHORO HUT

Hello, I'm Teboho. I live with my family in Lesotho in a small village of mokhoros. A mokhoro is a round hut built with stones, soil, and dung. The roof is thatched with grass so it's cool and dry in the summer.

MOKHORO

KITCHEN HUT

Our village is high up, so it gets dark early when the sun disappears behind the mountaintops. We have a light powered by a car battery, but in the daytime the doorway and our small window let in light and air. We eat and sleep in the mokhoro, all together. Ma used to cook in it, but now she has a separate smaller hut for that. It gets very smoky and hot!

BATTERY

Me and my sisters, Palesa and Bongi, help with tidying up, sweeping, cooking, milking the cows, and feeding the chickens. We grow potatoes, corn, and other vegetables. I used to have to carry containers of water for the garden in our wheelbarrow, but the village has a tap now.

WHERE: Lesotho, southern Africa

WHO: Two adults, three children

Mountainous Lesotho is nicknamed "The Kingdom in the Sky."

SOUTHERN BALD IBIS

TOILET HUT

The toilet's in another hut, and we flush it with a container of water. We get a lot of bugs in there, especially ants. Lots of ants.

BASOTHO BLANKET

MOKOROTLO HAT

When I'm not at school, I ride on horseback with Father, herding the sheep to pasture. We wear blankets to keep warm. I must go to school until I'm 13, but Father will decide if I can keep going. I study hard because I want to become a mechanic. Then I will buy a car and drive my children to school.

REFUGEE CAMP CARAVAN

I'm *Munira*, and I live in Jordan. My family is from Syria, but we had to leave our country because it's at war. We're refugees. Our home is a caravan without wheels in a camp called Za'atari.

My father fixed up the caravan so my brother Ibrahim and I have a small bedroom each. There's a tiny kitchen area, but we prefer cooking outside under a shady awning that we put up.

SUPERADOBE

The Za'atari camp was just tents at first, but now they're starting to construct "superadobe" buildings out of things like plastic sandbags, earth, and barbed wire. They'll resist floods and earthquakes, and they'll be cooler than metal caravans. We can't wait to live in one!

SOLAR POWER PLANT

WHERE: Jordan

WHO: Two adults and two children

Za'atari is the world's largest camp for Syrian refugees.

We have solar electricity, and Ibrahim and I can use the Internet. Our fresh water supply sometimes runs out and we can't wash. That's bad, because dust storms make everything filthy.

There are about 80,000 people in the camp. There's a long street with hundreds of businesses started by refugees—bakeries, grocery stores, and pizza takeouts. My father was a banker, but he's started a business here and works from home. He's "The Tech Doctor" and visits customers' homes to fix their devices.

My parents say we're the lucky ones, to have escaped the war, and we have doctors, dentists, and schools right here in Za'atari. They tell me to study hard so I can go to college and make a better life for myself, somewhere. I don't remember Syria, but I know it's a beautiful country. Everyone tells me so.

MEDICAL CENTER

HIGH-RISE APARTMENT

Hi! I'm Kiku. I live with my mother and my brother, Haru, in a tenth-floor manshon apartment in Tokyo, Japan.

Inside our front door there's a genkan—a section of floor that's slightly lower than the rest of the apartment. There we change into slippers before stepping up into the apartment. Visitors leave their shoes pointing toward the front door, so they're easy to slip on when they leave.

SHINJUKU GYOEN

GENKAN

Our kitchen, living, and dining room are one big space. Mama likes this because we can all chat or watch TV while she's cooking. There's a balcony, too. From there we can see Shinjuku Gyoen, my favorite park.

WHERE: Tokyo, Japan

WHO: One adult, two children

More people live in Tokyo than in any other city in the world—over 37 million.

When I sit at the desk beneath my bedroom window to do my homework, I look across at the National Stadium, and as the sun goes down, all of Tokyo lights up!

NATIONAL STADIUM

Our bathroom has a great bathtub. You can program its controls to set the water temperature and how deep you want it. Bath time is always perfect!

We have a traditional Japanese room called a washitsu. The floor is covered with tatami mats made with woven rushes. We never wear shoes or slippers in there. There's a cabinet with two futons stored inside for guests to sleep on when they visit.

TATAMI

Our building has extra things that all the residents share. Downstairs there's an exercise gym, which Mama uses every day. And on the very top of the building is the rooftop terrace, with plants and benches. It's a garden in the sky!

OLD FARMHOUSE

Hello. I'm Romy, from Bavaria in Germany. My mother isn't able to take care of me, so I live with my foster parents, Nina and Kristian, in their farmhouse.

Parts of the house are very old. The kitchen has a cooking range, and the first time I saw Nina open one of its doors, I was amazed to see a real fire inside! I love getting logs from the woodpile for the range and helping Nina bake bread. We usually eat in the kitchen—it's so warm.

COOKING RANGE

WHERE: Bavaria, southeast Germany

WHO: Two adults, one child, one horse, many other animals

Bavaria is the largest state in the country.

36

My bedroom is in an old part of the house. It has wooden beams across the ceiling. The floor slopes a bit and creaks, too. My bed is large and so comfy! I like being in my cozy room reading or playing games on my tablet.

SAANEN GOATS

I adore animals, so I love living on a farm. Nina has a flock of friendly goats, and I'm learning to milk them. The milk is sold to a neighbor who makes cheese. Ducks, geese, and chickens wander around the pond and through the barns and tractor shed, looking very busy. Kris takes care of the sheep and cows, and I groom Nina's horse. She's teaching me how to ride!

My friend lives two fields away. We made yellow flags, and when it's school time, we signal to each other from our windows, jump on our bikes, and meet at the end of the road. School's great, but I love going home to the farmhouse.

CAVE HOME

Hello, I'm Tafsut. I live with my parents, my brother, Usaden, and our three little sisters in a special underground home.

Our cave home is in Matmata, Tunisia. To make it, first a big, round pit was dug, then rooms were dug out around the edge of the pit, which became a courtyard. The doorways have little paintings above them. My handprint is there!

There's a well in the courtyard, so we don't have to go far for water. Our solar panels give us power for lights, a refrigerator, and—best of all—TV!

STORAGE ROOM

The kitchen has stone shelves for Mom's pottery dishes and whatever she needs for cooking. Some things are stored in upper rooms, but you need a ladder for those.

GOOD LUCK SYMBOLS

WELL

OLIVE GROVE

WHERE: Matmata, Tunisia

WHO: Two adults, five children, one kitten, and one dog

Matmata is on the edge of the Sahara desert, and the underground homes offer protection from extreme temperatures.

My cat, Mumu, sleeps on my bed, and Jappa the dog sleeps in Usaden's room, under his bed. Our mom wove our striped bedspreads. She weaves colorful rugs and cushion covers to sell, too.

We walk to school in Matmata's new town. Some of our neighbors moved there to live in ordinary houses. I don't want to move. I have brothers and sisters to play with, donkeys to ride, and plenty of space. We even have passageways linking our homes to other family members' homes, so I can be with my cousins in half a minute.

Fun fact! You might see an underground home like mine in a Star Wars movie. They filmed some of it right here!

HONAI HUT

Hello. I'm Noah, one of the Dani people of Highland Papua. My home in the Baliem Valley is a honai—a round hut made of wooden planks. The roof is thatched with palm leaves and slopes almost to the ground, like a shaggy hat!

Inside, the walls are lined with bamboo, and there's a fire pit in the middle for cooking and heat. The honai is roomy and very tall. A bamboo ladder leads to the upper floor, where Mami and me and my brother and sister sleep. When I'm older, I'll sleep in Papi's separate honai.

There's a fence around our huts, but we shut the pigs and chickens up at night so snakes and rats can't get them.

PALM LEAVES

For special feasts, we wrap meat and herbs in banana leaves and cook it on hot stones in a pit outside, in the area between our homes. Ooh, the delicious smell when it's opened up!

COOKING PIT

All children must go to school. Ours is in the town of Wamena, nearby. Papi says education will help us get jobs. I watch airplanes coming into Wamena, and I'd like to be a pilot. Many people work in the copper mines, like Uncle Joko, but I want something different.

SCHOOL

NOKEN BAG

People on vacation sometimes visit our village to see how we live. Mami earns money by selling bracelets and necklaces that she makes. Sometimes when tourists visit, we show them our traditional dress.

WHERE: Baliem Valley, Highland Papua, Indonesia

WHO: One adult, three children, pigs, and chickens

One family lives in a group of several honai.

TRADITIONAL YURT

WHERE: Kyrgyzstan

WHO: Two adults, three children, horses, sheep, and cattle

It takes just a few hours for an experienced person to assemble a yurt.

I'm Umar, from Kyrgyzstan, and I live in a yurt with my father, mother, and sisters, Amina and Safiya.

TUNDUK

We spend the winter down in the valley with our animals, and in the summer we all move to the jailoo, the high pastures.

A yurt is the easiest type of home to pack up and carry. Its frame is made from lightweight willow wood. Layers of thick felt go over it and are tied down with ropes. A hole at the top, called a tunduk, lets smoke out and light in. We burn animal dung on the fire in the middle of the yurt. It smells pretty nice when it's burning!

FELT

We're careful not to step on the wooden door frame as we enter the yurt.
We don't want bad luck! Inside, brightly colored carpets cover the floor.
The bags hanging on the walls were embroidered with yarn by Mom, and she's made
heaps of blankets and cushions to rest on. At night they're laid out for sleeping.

JAILOO

The left side of the yurt is for tools and animal
equipment. The right side is for food, dishes,
pans, spoons, and things we use for sewing. The
tea has its own wall bag. We drink so much of it!

Safiya and Amina help with the
milking, cooking, and cleaning.
I ride out with Dad to look after
our sheep (many) and cows (a few).
I love my horse. Her name is
Boroon, which means "storm." I
can't remember learning to ride. I
must have been very young.

HOUSEBOAT

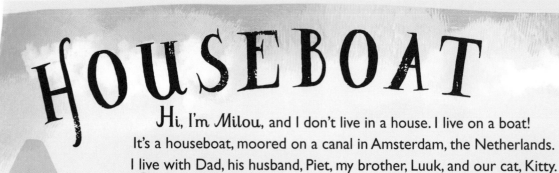

Hi, I'm Milou, and I don't live in a house. I live on a boat!
It's a houseboat, moored on a canal in Amsterdam, the Netherlands.
I live with Dad, his husband, Piet, my brother, Luuk, and our cat, Kitty.

There's a window seat in my little bedroom. When I was little, I stood on it, waving my wooden sword, pretending to be a pirate. Now I sit with Kitty, watching ducks with their ducklings, and geese waddling along the bank, hissing or honking crossly at everyone and everything.

HOUSE ARK

A swan sometimes visits early in the morning. He wakes us up by banging on the boat with his beak, asking for food!

There's always plenty to look at. Bicyclists whiz over the bridge nearby, and trams cross a bridge further along. All the time, boats sail up and down. If a silly sailor breaks the speed limit, it makes our houseboat rock. That annoys Piet when he's cooking!

Dad can't cook, but he's great at making and fixing things. I help him, so I'm learning how to care for our houseboat. We often help our neighbors, too.

After school, Luuk and I cross the gangplank into the kitchen and sniff the freshly baked cake or cookies Piet has usually made for us! We flop onto the sofa to eat them and watch TV while Dad works at his desk.

At night, I open my curtains to see people strolling past or having fun at canal-side café tables. I wouldn't want to live anywhere else.

WHERE: Amsterdam, the Netherlands

WHO: Two adults, two children, one cat

Some of Amsterdam's 2,400 houseboats are floating boats, and others, called house arks, are fixed in place.

GANGPLANK

RAIL LINE BUILDING APARTMENT

Hi, I'm Yan Ya. I live in an eleventh-floor apartment in the city of Chongqing, China, with my parents and 14 tropical fish.

My mother jokes about having to walk a long way to catch the train to work, because it couldn't be any closer. There's a rail station on the sixth to eighth floors below us, and the train goes right through our building!

MONORAIL

The structure that holds the rail line up is separate from the part that holds the building up, and the train runs on rubber tires. It's so quiet, we don't notice it! People on the ninth floor say it's no noisier than their dishwasher!

WHERE: Chongqing, China

WHO: Two adults, one child, 14 fish

This apartment building is unique in the world.

When my friends come home with me, we stand at the living room window to watch the train whiz into view around the bend. They squeal when it heads straight for us!

We usually eat at the kitchen table, but every Wednesday, when my aunt and uncle come, we use the table in our big living room. Mom often cooks Chinese hot pot. It's very spicy, and it's put in the middle of the table so we can help ourselves. Everyone loves hot pot!

STATION

My bedroom window looks over the Jialing River, which joins the Yangtze River in Chongqing. I love watching the boats while I do my homework. At night, I lie in bed and gaze at the city lights, and I dream of what I'll be when I grow up. Not a train driver or a rail line worker . . . I'm going to be an architect, designing amazing buildings!

JIALING RIVER

INDEX